EMERSON
AND HIS BEST FRIEND
YET

Written by Jennifer Lynne Kennard

Illustrated by Andrias Taniwan

EMERSON
AND HIS BEST FRIEND
YET

To my patient Emerson, my sweet Annie, and my supportive husband, Bradford - for ALWAYS being kind and NEVER giving up.

Hi, my name is Yet.

This is Emerson. Have you met?

Emerson is my best friend.

I'm by his side now, and I've been there when...

I simply answered, "Emerson don't fret."

"Tying your shoes takes patience and practice.
I know you'll get it, if you just keep at it."

Just like the time he learned to ride his bike.

and before he knew it, those tears turned to fun!

And what about that day, I'll never forget.

He threw down that book and shouted,
"I CAN'T DO IT, YET!"

So together we sounded out the "q-u's" and "b-a's"...

he never gave up,
until he could read every page.

Then there was that summer,
all the kids went to the lake.

He said, "I can't do it, Yet!" because he was afraid.

Afraid, he couldn't swim,
and the kids would all laugh...

but look at him now,
in the pool ahead of the pack.

So, when you feel frustrated because your knots should be loops, and you'd rather put on your old Velcro shoes.

With a little patience and practice...

LOVE, YET!

www.ingramcontent.com/pod-product-compliance
Lightning Source LLC
Chambersburg PA
CBHW041323290426

44108CB00004B/118